CLAIM IT!

DON'T BLAME IT!

A LOGICAL ADULT'S GUIDE TO HAPPINESS

BY **RAY "LEFTY" RHODES**

ISBN: 978-1-948638-08-1

Visit my website at:

www.girlzrstoopidandboyzrduhm.com

REAL
REALITY
PUBLISHING

LeftyMancino LeftyMancino
leftymancino@gmail.com

AUTHOR'S NOTE TO THE READER

Before you start reading,
I truly recommend reading my book
Girlz R S-too-pid & Boyz R Duh-m.

Doing this first will prepare you
to get the most benefit from

Claim it! Don't Blame it!

Visit your favorite online retailer
to get your copy today. or visit my website:

www.girlzrstoopidandboyzrduhm.com

ACKNOWLEDGMENTS

Shout out to my best friend for being the first example of (me seeing) someone claim ALL of their mistakes, faults and shortcomings instead of blaming anything in their life on anybody else! Amazingly, after one very long conversation, she was able to stop cold turkey from cigarettes, pills, and alcohol! Now, she owns her own business! She has now been operating independently for almost a decade now. I'm so proud of you little honey bunny, much love and appreciation for always showing that courage and support with constant reminders of greatness!

I have to acknowledge the man that made me fearless in all aspects.

The big mac himself, my big cousin Ronald Morris aka 6 aka Big Ron of the Morris boys clan, who also taught me not to claim anything (as far as gangs and associations) but my last name! I appreciate you and am gonna miss those Sunday meals and great conversations, jokes, and overall great times at your place.

R.I.P. lol give the devil hell!

DEDICATION

This book is dedicated to the woman who always told me "Keep God in front of you and the devil behind. Nothing and nobody can get in ya way, slow you down, or stop you!" Then she'd say, "Think about it, REALLY THINK ABOUT IT! lol She always said it twice! She was the only person I knew in my family to get her own house built from the ground up, as well as being the only Catholic that I knew in our family.

She taught me what positive and justifiable righteous pride was. As in, to have pride in who you are because of your morals, values, education and skill set, as opposed to being proud of your looks or material possessions. Definitely not pride in what others thought!

I was also named after her first and only son, who died while my mom was pregnant with me.

Plus, her baby sister (who's my grandmother) was married to my grandfather in which had become her good buddy, pal, friend and her own brother whom she and she only called Rooney lol while others called him Mickey!

She was a loving, hardworking, dedicated beacon of positive light and sternness. An Angel who truly got her wings! Enjoy heaven, Ant Annie Miles (born Ann Morris) I'll always love and remember you!

Angels here and there,
she armed herself with her weapons
now an angel has earned her wings
and has made it into heaven
may her lessons be learned and her lessons be taught
blessed be what she left here & may it never rot
white people, black people, money is green
I too will be working until my knees bleed,
then get up and lick 'em clean!

RIH to my Aunt Ann She was a true example of whoever you are and whatever you do baby, claim it, don't blame it!

PREFACE

A rich and very wealthy man looked around himself and saw misery and self-doubt everywhere. He got tired of being asked the same questions: How can you possibly always be happy? Have you always been happy? What's the secret to your success and happiness?

One day, he'd had enough. He jumped up and screamed, "Are you in a bad mood or bad situation?! Having a bad day, week, month, year or life? Well, who's fault is it?

"WAIT Whose life is it?

"Oh, the same answer to multiple totally different questions!

"I'll show ya.

"OK, if anything is bad in your life, I bet someone else is involved. Think about it!

"OK, now focus on what you can change about yourself and your situation. NOW you're working toward a goal and that's your right!!!

"Boys and girls, men and women of America, please let me inform and remind you all that we have the right to the pursuit of happiness!

"This is where the pursuit begins! Welcome to team No Excuses!

"I know you've heard these two familiar phrases: shit happens and life's a bitch. Well, keep those two in mind, because they are both true and fitting, which is why they are common sayings! Admittedly, yes, bad things happen to good people and nobody can explain why their god would bless or allow bad or evil people to have riches and wealth. They also can't explain why some babies catch stray bullets, and all the other bad things that happen every day. So, I suggest you focus on yourself, *your* peace and *your* happiness by harnessing all the positivity you can and taking control of every situation. Take charge in life. Start claiming your life, not blaming anything or anyone else anymore!

"It's all up to you — so claim it, don't blame it!

WHAT ARE CLAIMING
AND BLAMING?

Claim: an assertion of something as a fact
Blame: assigning responsibility for a fault or wrong.

Dictionary.com defines claim as: an assertion of something as a fact/to assert and demand the recognition of (a right, title, possession, etc.); assert one's right to claim payment for services.

The same source defines blame as: to place the responsibility for (a fault, error, etc.) usually followed by on, for example: I blame the accident on her.

Therefore, to claim anything or blame anything, you first have to acknowledge that you are aware of the evidence, fact, truth or experience (problem) that you are referring to when you are claiming or blaming said instance. This could be a plethora of possibilities, but we'll stick to things I know about and have conquered myself in the upcoming chapters.

Please remember the whole time you're reading, the reason for claiming and not blaming is simply to achieve your own happiness. Doing this will lead to your overall success and will make your world a better place!

If you are a better YOU every day, and you assist and/or inspire everyone you are around, then they will do the same, guaranteeing that the world will indeed be a better place.

So, let's start now, with ourselves. Let's all claim it, don't blame it!

INTRODUCTION

In this book, I plan to show people the picture of productivity and positive progression, which could be their future life if they are willing to claim all that holds them back from a happy and successful future instead of blaming it on their unchangeable past or others.

After reading this book, my goal is for you all to aim high, reach those heights, and raise your expectations in life and your level of happiness with yourself and your life. I pray, like always, that this book makes the reader a better and happier person. I hope they learn to value self-investments, and begin to contribute to the world, working to make it a happier, and therefore a better, place.

Amen (so be it)!

TABLE OF CONTENTS

CHAPTER 1

YOUR PAST

L et me start by saying that I'm a very cine-
matic thinker. A lot of movies start off with
the main character being grown. The narra-
tor asks where they should start, then says, "The
beginning, of course." So, let's just start with the
beginning — any problem you have in your past.
Yes, your past is where all problems start. Were you
raped? Did you have a sad childhood? Were you
lonely, abused, traumatized? On the flip side, did
you have a ideal, happy love-filled childhood?

Either way you look at it, your past shapes your
future. You have to understand the polarization of
feelings on the subject and how this will affect your
ability to relate to and be relatable to others. A lot
of people make the mistake of using their past as
a measure for acceptance, goals, and/or happiness.
I say that's a mistake, because as a child, you could

not understand the significance of decisions that were made for, or put on, you by adults and other influences in your young life. Now, you have these habits, hobbies, turn ons/offs, quirks, likes/dislikes, religion/other beliefs, traditions, etc. that might not fit who you really are now as an adult. It's up to you to take control of your life and change what you don't like about it and yourself.

You have to be honest with yourself first — that's a major key to this process. The first step is admittance. After you're honest enough to admit what you don't like about yourself or what's holding you back from getting what you want or where you want to be, then and only then will you be able to fix things about yourself. You can't fix a flaw that you don't, can't or refuse to see!

If you don't like how your body looks/feels, then change what you eat to nutritious food, like electric foods, and start a workout regimen. Soon, you'll like the way you look and feel!

Side notes:

- *Electric Foods include avocados, bell peppers, cactus flowers, chickpeas, cucumbers, dandelion greens, kale, lettuce (except iceberg), mushrooms (except shiitake), okra, olives, sea vegetables, squash, tomatoes (cherry and plum only), zucchini, fonio, amaranth, Khorasan wheat (kamut), rye, wild rice, spelt, teff, and quinoa.)*

- *Don't forget to stay hydrated, ingest the proper daily vitamins, minerals, and sleep regularly :-)*

Yes, it's that simple. Plan the work and then work the plan, as my uncle Kip always told me growing up!

Instead of blaming your current situation on your past, you should claim it and understand how you were shaped. Once you do that, you can move forward by searching for and getting your own information to better yourself. In my book *Girlz R S-too-pid & Boyz R Duh-m,* I explain how and why it's important to invest in yourself. Some people had their "reasons" (cough: excuses) why they couldn't do this, and things that were still stopping them from being grown and taking charge

3

and control of their situations. Claim your past and better your future. Once you've done that, you can avoid being influenced by others who want you to do things that aren't in your best interest.

If you don't know what I mean by claiming your past, look at it like a felon. When the felon first gets out of jail or prison they are on probation or parole for a certain period of time. During that time, they have to stay sober, be law abiding citizens, find and keep employment, and not have any association with any other offenders. If you've violated or have been violated, this is you getting out of the jail or prison of your past. Get rid of all that reminds you of the imprisonment.

This starts with evaluating your mindset, then the people, places and things in your life. You also have to pay attention to your past and the things that may have triggered you, stunted your growth and/or influenced your feelings in good or bad ways. Don't look for who's at fault, and don't moan about how you were victimized. Instead, understand how strong you are for overcoming whatever you have been through and use that strength to move on. Let confidence build the bridge to get you over things, but once the water is under the bridge don't look back. It's just that, water under a bridge.

Now, go back to that same felon scenario. We have all heard, seen on TV, or know someone who uses their felony as an excuse to not get a job, education, career, own a company or do anything else to better their situation. There are also felons that move forward with a job, but are still shackled to their past. They brag on the glory days, and never move forward and truly appreciate the position they're currently in. They have no chance at their best future, because they never fully invest in their present because they're too busy looking back at the past.

Something else I'd like you to think about is how far and how fast can you go forward if you're constantly looking back?! Have you ever driven to a destination by looking in the rear view mirror the whole way there? I'm not talking about checking the mirror, I mean looking nonstop in the rear view while driving forward. That's definitely the hardest way to get anywhere, if you can do it at all!

This is the point of claiming your past and not blaming your current situation on events that have already happened that you can't change! The thing about the past you need to always remember is — you can't change it! It already happened!

So, where and who are you right now? What don't you like about yourself? Are you willing to change it? I already said if you don't like your body then change it, same goes for your job, education level and bank account balance! It especially goes for the company you keep, the people you surround yourself with and your allowed group of influences.

Your journey toward change all starts with getting new information! You have to learn something new to do something new, and you'll have to do something you've never done before to find something new for yourself that you've never had before! Changing is a lot of work, and it's never easy, but you have to keep your eyes on the prize!

What is your goal? It should be to be the best you that you can be — mind, body, and spirit.

What if you don't like the fact that you have kids?! Are you willing to give them up for adoption or send them to live with their other parent or family members? My point in going there is to make you think about and understand what options you have available that are acceptable by your own standards!

Calm down! I'm not telling you to get rid of your kids. However, you should think about what's best for you and them and be honest with yourself. If you are not the best person to raise them or if you don't feel you're capable, then make the decision to give the best life possible, even if that's not with you.

Sometimes, we bite off more than we're able to chew and can feel like we're barely staying afloat and are about to drown. Many times, all we have to do is lighten our load to survive and get to our destination — happiness. You have to get to happiness before you can get anywhere else, because all other destinations are pointless if you don't have happiness.

Now, what this does is build what people call self-esteem. Once your self-esteem is untouchable, then you'll have the confidence and honesty to know what mountains you can climb, which ones you can move, and which ones you'll need help with. There's only so much you can do by yourself, but that amount is a lot, so do everything you can for yourself and by yourself. These things include education, diet, working out, and getting money!

You are the only one guaranteed to be in your future. Remember that tomorrow isn't promised to any of us, so live now and do the most that you can.

You know how much sleep you need, so don't blame being tired on anything but you not taking care of yourself. Don't "get time," make time!

Either deal with or let go of your past. Once you've caught up with yourself mentally, and know what you don't like about your present that comes from your past, see what you can do about it and then do it!

Reference the serenity prayer:

God, grant me the serenity to accept the things I cannot change, courage to change the things I can, and wisdom to know the difference.

In my opinion, understanding that prayer is all you need to know to be able to deal with your past. You can't change the events, but you can dictate the outcome. That was your past, and this is your present life, so...

CHAPTER 2

ADDICTION

Now that we understand that our past is something that we didn't choose, we are on the right track to claiming and not blaming by accepting. Accepting what we chose, what was put on us, and what we can change now.

So today, you are grown, you are an adult! With that said, now it's all up to you to choose the best things for you in order for you to be the best you that you can be.

I briefly mentioned a proper diet of nutritious electric foods in the first chapter of this book because the first thing we can choose is what we put into our bodies. Let's keep it positive and focus on what we should be putting in our bodies first. By focusing on the positive, you can intentionally avoid making excuses.

I'll give you a quick personal story just so you can understand that I have empathy while listening to a personal horror story about bad parenting, being victimized, being left with no choices, all of which eventually lead to drug addiction. People say that because I've never used drugs, I can't understand addiction. I've been addicted to a lot of destructive objects, people and lifestyles, so I do understand. Here's one of my stories:

I worked at the top mortgage broker in my state when I started. The company was and 17th in the nation then, and was 3rd in the nation by the time the bubble popped. There were two buildings at this company — one where the loan officers and underwriters, where they brought in clients, and the other where the assistant loan officers and telemarketers worked.

The lady who was my manager when I was working as a telemarketer had a mouth full of rotten teeth, but she was a really happy and cool person. She was passionate and a hard worker, and it turned out she was a great manager.

As I pulled myself up in the company ranks, I was often invited to go out to eat and the company paid for my meals. That progressed to drinks out, then partying, and house gatherings, boating, and lake outings, and so on and so forth.

One night, Sarah, the manager with the messed-up teeth, asked me if I could give her a ride home, and I kindly obliged. On the way to drop her off, she said, "I know you smoke weed, and I'd love some right now." That was when I knew I could ask her about her teeth! I rolled up and I lit it. Then, as soon as I handed it to her I said, "Sooooo Sarah, I got two questions for you."

She hit it lightly and said, "I know what you're gonna ask. First, I don't usually smoke blunts and that's why I don't know how to roll. Next, you wanna know about my teeth, right?"

I said, "Damn. How you know?"

She said, "Well number one, we're smoking weed, and everybody always wants to know about my teeth."

She told me the story of how for five years (when she was seven up until about the age of twelve) her mom used to use and abuse all kinds of drugs. When she smoked crack and meth, she would stare at her only child and ask, "What are you looking at, you little bitch? You think you're better than me?!" then punch her in the stomach (and sometimes the mouth). Then she would shove and hold the pipe in her mouth.

Finally, when she was 12, the school picked up on the fact that she was an addict, and they took her into state custody. Her mom is clean now, but has permanent mental damage and gets a disability check from the state. Sarah's mom lives with her, and she takes care of her mom and her own two kids that she got back from the state. She's been clean herself for eight years (at that time) and has had them for three years.

She was saving money to get her teeth done, because our employer didn't have dental insurance. She was saving the cash and she had just got her passport so she could go to Mexico and get them fixed for half price.

I went from feeling sorry for Sarah to being proud of her. Point being, I don't judge the origin story of your addiction, I focus on the bigger picture of health. Sarah didn't have a choice in her addiction, but she took control and bettered her life! She took responsibility and became able to help her mom and her children after helping and bettering herself. If Sarah can do it, so can you!

Sarah claimed and understood her problem, then decided to grow up and solve it, instead of blaming it on the past and others! The truly beautiful part of this story is how loving and forgiving she turned out to be after choosing to care about and invest in herself.

There are two things I'll tell you about addiction: if you can recognize it, then you can change it; and when you realize it isn't helping you get to your goal, then you should stop. Those are two pieces of advice that will only be effective if you are being honest with yourself! So, what are your goals and what's helping you or hindering you from accomplishing them?

Health is Wealth

Focus on the best quality of life that you can live, because relatively speaking, humans are only here on earth for a short time. There are many plants, animals and other living organisms on this planet that far outlive humans, so be excited to live, see and be better every day! Live better by being healthier, and know that addiction is not healthy.

The first step to claiming a better life, instead of blaming the life you live on others, is being the best you that you can be! The first step to being the best is bettering yourself. The first step to bettering yourself is to be the healthiest you can be, which means only putting healthy, necessary things into your body such as electric foods and alkaline water to ensure your body gets the proper nutrients and hydration, which will allow your brain, heart and lungs the correct amount of oxygen and blood.

After doing this, you've eliminated poison (alcohol and drugs) and you're finally guaranteeing you'll be totally in your right mind.

Now three quick things I'll tell you about bettering yourself are:

1. If you knew better you could do better.

2. When you know better, then you're supposed to show better!

3. Last, but definitely not least, now that you can see better you can and should *be* better!

When I was in my early twenties, I unfortunately got a DUI. I went to an alcohol education class and found out that OVER 90% of people on drugs were introduced to them by the opposite sex. That taught me that most people on drugs blame (other people) the opposite sex.

Welcome, again, to Team NO Excuses!

Around that time in my life, I also learned how acceptable it was to blame others for our problems. In bars, I often heard guys blaming the president or the government for their woes, and it makes me think back to a lot of senior citizens complaining back in the day, about the war, pensions and raising the minimum age for social security. My point is, your addiction, no matter who's fault it may be, is YOUR problem. It's got to be YOUR choice to whether YOU continue down this destructive path or YOU quit.

Don't blame something or someone else, or wait on others to do something before you decide to reach healthy sobriety. With a proper diet and workout plan, while maintaining adequate hydration and sleep, you may find out that you don't even need prescription drugs either. You can solve a lot of your own problems with a healthy lifestyle and mentality — so try it.

Think about it like this, if nothing else you know what it's like to get high and drunk while eating fast food. Now, let's just see how and what you can be by trying a different approach and see which way leads you to where you want to be. You might just find yourself accomplishing the actual goals that you set.

I guarantee you'll enjoy food and sex a lot more when you're sober, but that's just the icing on the pound cake, if you get my drift. Flowers will smell better when you rid your body of toxins and mucus. Life will be better and you'll be better in life by being able to focus more, have more energy and less pain — and, of course, you'll be happier.

Think about it like this, even if you don't like the healthy, sober lifestyle after 60 days then you'll be so clean that when you go back (if you choose to) it'll be like it's the first time again. Lower tolerance equals stronger effects, so at least reset your system, cuz that's the one thing about being healthy — it can't hurt!

You've made it this far, and you should now be able to understand how and why you should and could claim your addiction and not blame it!

CHAPTER 3

RELATIONSHIPS

A fter you have claimed your past and addictions, now you have nobody else to blame for the way that you choose to deal with other people. You can't deal with new people in a manner that reflects or is in response (retaliation) to people in your past, or those that were involved in your life when you indulged in addiction. How you treat the cashier, your new date or family has to be in accordance to their behavior and experiences with you, directly and personally.

I'll elaborate: don't "look for clues" that someone is cheating or assume that two different people with the same behavior have the same intentions or even the same knowledge. Communication is truly key. Whether it's dealing with relationships or just a simple conversation, you need to be able to inform people correctly about what you want, need, like or find unacceptable, offensive or disre-spectful! Always speak up and stand up for yourself.

Claim your desires and frustrations as well as who you are or aren't interested in. Then you'll be able to tell someone why you like or dislike something as well. If you've read *Girlz R S-too-pid & Boyz R Duh-m,* then you already know yourself and why you like what you like. Now you've come to the point where you take it to the next level by claiming what you like sexually or partner-wise, instead of blaming the person who did or didn't do it for you in your previous relationships.

For instance, don't say things like, "I had an ex who used to love going down on me but was no good at it," and then laugh… it's not funny, it's awkward. What's the other person supposed to respond with, an equally distasteful joke or phony laugh?!

I also said in *Girlz R S-too-pid & Boyz R Duh-m,* don't compare! When you have a friend or lover, don't compare them to anyone else, because it comes off seeming like you're blaming the one you're with for not being like the one you used to be with, or even the porn star on the screen. Porn stars go on special diets, take certain pills, enemas, have body waxing and record multiple takes that are edited, so please understand that it is their job to present to you what you see, not to actually please each other.

The person you are with is not an actor/ actress and neither are you. Claim what you like and don't blame them for not knowing what that is or doing it without being told what you want. Make people aware of what you want or like, but don't expect them to do it just because you've made them aware.

I've been around and talked to a lot of males and females that have confided in me about their love lives, friendships and flings, as well as their marriages and reasons for divorce. This is what prompted me to add this chapter to the book.

Often times in relationships, people look for what they think of as red flags. Well there's a saying that I feel applies to this, and it goes like this: "If you look for something hard enough, you're bound to find it!" With that said, don't focus on negativity or be so quick to judge someone on behavior that might seem similar to others you've dealt with in your past. Everyone is an individual. So, if you claim to be an individual, then treat the person you're dealing with as an individual too.

Just because you know someone who has a stutter and lies all the time, doesn't mean that everybody who stutters is a liar. lol Seriously, salt and sugar only look the same. If your ex only popped up at your job when he needed to use your car, that doesn't mean that your new guy is going to act the same way. When he shows up at your job, he's there just to take you out for lunch (even if he did get dropped off or had to catch the bus or take a cab to get there). Respect the individual and be respectable as an individual.

I don't agree with treating others as you want to be treated, because others aren't you. That means they won't want what you want or how you want it. As the great Dave Chappelle said "Some people think cucumbers taste better pickled!" Some people prefer high-top Air Force Ones to lows, and others love mids — but some people don't even like Nikes! Point being, treat people how they ask you to treat them, and if they don't deserve your presence or don't return the respect and understanding, then don't have them in your life. Yes, it is that simple!

Being comfortable in and with yourself is a major key to happiness and in return, your happiness will provide you with confidence and a healthy self-esteem. Therefore, you won't have trust issues or have a problem seeing your value. You'll appreciate what you have, instead of feeling pressured to hold onto something or someone you don't want or worse, someone who doesn't want you. You'll know that the individual you are dealing with is dealing with you because you are you, and nobody else can be you. This will provide you with peace.

By claiming and being who you are as an individual, you won't end up blaming your relationship failures on others, so-called frenemies (fake friends who are really your enemies), competition (yours or their family, kids), the economy, the government, race, religion or anybody or anything else. Claim your victories and faults instead of blaming the elements, the universe, God and or "the haters."

Like I mentioned in *Girlz R S-too-pid & Boyz R Duh-m,* once you're happy with and by yourself, then it makes it possible to be happy with and/or around others as well. You should have a positive, energetic vibe at work so coworkers, customers and clients want to be around you. They want to see you because of the wonderful, positive vibes and energy radiating and flowing from you.

Just as a fun fact: like laughter, smiles are contagious (even through the phone)! Being good company will almost guarantee you'll find yourself in the midst of good company as well.

Goals

This brings me back to goals. Happy people will support their loved ones, if nothing else by giving encouraging words and free promos or referrals. The people you surround yourself with will do the same. Now we're talking about creating a happily successful networking community! It all starts with knowing yourself and being yourself, then bettering yourself and perfecting your craft. With education and experience of and with self, you can now introduce yourself as an individual who is interested in living a healthy life and focusing on your goal (whatever it is).

Once you get to this point in life, the law of attraction will make itself known to you, and you will notice that like-minded people, good company, mentors and others interested in investing in you will come to your aid and help you to reach your goals. Happy will become your reality.

The Winner's Circle

Being in the winner's circle, as I call it, will provide you with a clear view of the opportunities and choices in front of you, and what you choose will shape your future and choose the people in it with you. During this development, your attention will be captured by a reoccurring character that familiarity builds with, and love will find you.

Love shouldn't be a requirement or goal for a relationship. All relationships, whether personal or professional, should start with the base principles of friendship. I've found that it's impossible to have a happy and successful relationship without real friendship as the foundation. So, operating under that logic, I encourage you to build your foundations in friendship whenever you decide to invest in any relationship.

I call it investing, because that's what you're doing. You're spending time, giving of yourself in the form of attention, and probably money, all with the expectation of a return. Let me give you some examples. If you smile at the cashier who's ringing up your purchases, then you expect to get a smile back. When you say thank you, then you expect the other person to say you're welcome. If you sneeze, you expect people to say God bless you and everyone expects others to say excuse me when they pass gas in either direction (through their mouth or posterior) in public.

My point is, don't devalue yourself by not counting your time and attention as investments.

You could be investing that time and attention in learning a new language or skill online for free, rather than trying to build a relationship with someone! Hopefully you can understand why it's so imperative that you invest in yourself and your happiness first and foremost. You need to be the best you can be if you want to be able to relate to and be relatable to others. If you don't build that foundation, then remember that misery loves company!

Choose Wisely

You are heavily influenced by the five people closest to you — the ones you communicate with on a regular basis. Obviously, these people are important to your happiness, so choose wisely. Think of the saying: "Teamwork makes the dream work" when choosing who you want in your life. There's only so much one person can do by themselves. Being healthy, positive and goal oriented will help you to build a like-minded team of friends.

Doing this will guarantee your pathway leads you to success and happiness as an individual.

If you read my first book *Girlz R S-too-pid & Boyz R Duh-m,* there's no way you will allow yourself to be in any relationship, especially a romantic one, with someone who doesn't at least know themselves and is capable of functioning as an independent, grown-up adult. There is no way you'll be successful if you're constantly forced to deal with people who refuse to grow up and take responsibility for themselves.

So, now that you've realized these things, you're open to meeting new people and building a solid foundation of happiness because you've chosen to claim your past, admit your addictions, and seen your bad relationships for what they are. You're ready to be a grown-up who, instead of blaming things on others making your problem everybody else's problem, is willing to take responsibility for yourself, your actions and your choices.

You're on your way to being able to communicate with others and maintain your happiness, which will put you in a position to be ready for love. Your self-realization will make you ready to share love and accept love, because your priorities are already in line and your foundation is secure. I would say that you're ready to build your network of positivity by investing in the right relationships.

So, remember, when it comes to relationships …

CHAPTER 4

LOVE AND SUCCESS

I put love and success in the same chapter because, for a lot of people they go hand in hand. What I mean by that is, some people think of love as success. Getting back to the idea of investments, some people work hard at love and for love. After they have put so much into that love or lover, they, too, expect a return on their investment. Whether it be in the form of a key to your place, a label for friends, family, public and society, or a ring on the finger, it feels good to be rewarded with a promise or a gesture showing you that your hard work is paying off and is appreciated. Meanwhile others, who love their jobs, look for raises in pay, promotions, or elevated positions such as manager or supervisor, as well as receiving accolades for their sacrifices and displays of loyalty and dependability.

The sad part of this can be sacrificing one love in favor of the other because you just can't find a way to be happy and balance both. As I taught you in my first book, happiness comes from within and it's impossible to have it with anyone else until you know and have it yourself. You can't be happy with others if you're not happy with yourself!

Let it Go!

The first step to happiness is honesty — honesty with others and honesty with yourself! You first have to claim what you want for yourself, whether your goal is romantic love, career success or both. This is why I started this book off saying you should start with your past, but when it comes to claiming your love, you should also start with the *truth* about your past.

How much of the failure in your love life are you blaming on your past? Let that blame go right now. If someone hurt you and you cannot forgive them, then don't have them in your life. Also remember, just because you choose to forgive them doesn't mean that you have to keep them in your life. I know you've heard it before but I totally agree that some people are in your life for a reason and some are there for just a season. Live and let go — that's' the only way to find what's out there for you.

Yes, we make mistakes, maybe spending more time or taking extra steps with someone we should have left sooner, but we don't have to keep living with that regret. Regret leads to depression. You don't wanna be depressed, so don't live with regret.

Live and let die is what I always say. Don't look for revenge or wait for someone to right their wrongs against you, just keep it pushing because success is the greatest revenge. To get more in depth I'll give you an example: if someone cheats on you, then don't cheat on them to get back at them. Also, don't wait to get more proof or punish them, because you're only prolonging the pain for yourself — you cannot make someone respect or value you by punishing them for the wrongs they've done to you. If it hurts that bad then just let the whole situation go!

Focus!

Focus on positivity and achieving your happiness. Your own happiness has to be the main priority in your life. When it is, then you will love yourself and accept others in your life who also love you. When you are loving and caring for yourself properly, then it's easy to see those who mean you harm, don't love you or simply just don't have your best interests in mind. You'll soon get to a point where you won't allow people to negatively affect your love, and then success will follow automatically.

How can I be so sure, you ask? Because when you truly care for and love yourself, you'll be the healthiest that you can be and you just won't allow unhealthy things or people into your life. You'll only want to be around those who have yours and their own best interests in mind.

Another benefit of loving yourself is taking pride in your appearance — good hygiene, an attractive appearance and healthy habits will definitely result in more opportunities that will make it hard to not be successful. See why I'm so sure now?!

Please believe me, I know it's not fun to do the same thing every day, no matter how much you enjoy it, but you have to keep in mind the end result. People don't wanna go to the gym every day or diet, sacrificing the delicious things they'd like to eat, but living longer with a higher quality of life is why they continue to do it.

A determined athlete starts training in childhood when their goal is to get all the way to the pros — they are always focused on the end result. What's your end result? If you want to be CEO, a supervisor, or happily married, the question and process is still the same. As my uncle Derek Rhodes, aka Kip, has always told all of us: "You plan the work, then you work the plan!" That's the way it is for everything in life including love and success.

Now that you understand a little better, let's expand on it so that it's completely clear. First, an in-depth example of happiness in love — love yourself by caring for yourself and leading by example. While loving yourself, you will be setting an example for others, showing them how to love and respect you.

You will be able to recognize real love from another by the understanding that you get and give for/by yourself to yourself. My book *Girlz R S-too-pid & Boyz R Duh-m* teaches you about the importance of self-investment and self-love, plus how and why it's so important when dealing with others.

Accept your past experiences and past loves and know that you can't change anything in the past. You can just collect the experiences and claim what you like and want, while being able to accept the past hurt and use it as an experience and proof of what you don't like in a relationship. The key is to not blame anything on anybody else because, for one, it's over, and second, blame won't make it any better. So, realize it happened and now you need to move on without the negativity and hurt in our life — even if that means the people who caused you the pain are no longer in your life!

Don't blame your current actions and thoughts on your past either, because that's unfair to the present. You have to be able to live and learn, but you can't dwell on the past because the more time you spend looking back the less time you have to look forward — and that's where you're going! You can't travel back to the past and change it, so stop looking back there. Move on!

Now, on to success. If you keep thinking about all the past things that happened and the obstacles you feel are against you, and you complain that the powers that be won't or don't help you, then you won't be able to recognize all the help and positivity out there waiting for you in the world.

Consider this example: you blame society or the president or your record on why you don't have what you want or need, instead of looking for ways to get it! Plenty places hire felons, and there are a lot of companies that entrepreneurs can start up with no money, not to mention the unlimited resources to be found on the internet — if you don't have the internet at home, get a free library card and use theirs! It's nobody else's fault that you choose to not work.

So, get grown, and find a solution to whatever problem you have that's blocking your success. Invest more time in loving yourself, and others will start investing more in you as well. Remember, you can't help someone until they help themselves. In this case, the someone is you! You get what you go for! This is America and this is your life, so claim your love and your success and get out there —

CHAPTER 5

FINANCES

inances are tricky. I say that because there is such a thing as a financial education. In America, we are all mostly financially illiterate. If you don't feel like you are, like I mentioned in the previous chapter, in America we have FREE libraries WITH the internet AND unlimited books and HELP at these facilities — plus there are FREE computers there for you to use! So, in my opinion nobody has an excuse for financial ignorance.

To learn banking, talk to a banker, read banking articles or research banking websites and companies. It takes some work, but the name of this book is not *Life in America is Easy* — NO its *Claim it Don't blame it!* So, let's claim our financial situation right now. As Grant Cardone says in his book *Be Obsessed or Be Average,* either work toward your dream or someone will hire you to work toward theirs. Now, let me say that there is nothing wrong with working for someone else. But ask yourself, why am I working for someone else? This is what we have to claim — our choices, decisions and our past that lead us to where we are today.

Claim your past, but don't blame it. In other words, don't complain about your job or your pay and make excuses like lack of a degree or other education keeping you from making things better for yourself. Like I'm hopefully making clear to you by now, that's your past and it's time to stop blaming it, and claim a new future for yourself by making some changes.

The point of claiming your past is to see where you can fix things or let them go. If you lack education and keep blaming your lack of options on this fact, claim your G.E.D. Don't blame child support for the reason you're not working or don't have a driver's license or have warrants. Instead, claim your situation, identify the problems and work toward the solutions.

Don't blame your boss for not giving you a raise or a promotion. Instead, claim the position and work for the job you want, not the job you have. Remember that a closed mouth does not get fed. So, make known what you're working for and find out what it takes to get what you want, and whether it's even available to you. Everything isn't for everybody, and everybody isn't for everything. I said what I said! If your goal is unrealistic, redirect your efforts to another goal that is more obtainable. ALWAYS be real with yourself!

Claim a Better Mindset

We have to claim our shortcomings and poor decisions before we can claim a better mindset and build a better life. I don't have to beat on you all with a long list of unnecessary purchases that we all make instead of sacrificing and saving, or at least making more profitable investments. Yeah, look around at all the *stuff* you have but don't need. Think about what you've spent on the clothes and shoes you bought to wear to the club, the cigarettes, cigars, alcohol, restaurant meals, expensive vacations, nights out, unnecessary days off etc. Like

I said, I'm not trying to beat you over the head with redundant examples, but I do want you to be honest with yourselves about why your financial situation isn't what you want it to be, instead of blaming your kids, your exes or past relationships, your skin color, the banks, our president, our state, our parents, the universe, another life or God!

It's easy to say, "If I hit the lottery, if I was born into money, if I won a lawsuit, I would be better off." Well my response is to look up how many people hit the lottery for millions and then were bankrupt in less than five years. Understand that the second you choose to look for an excuse or someone else to blame for why you don't have something, you are taking away from the time, energy and attention you could be using to solve your problem by arming yourself with more information on the subject so you can get closer to your goals.

Goals

Speaking of goals, what are yours?! Financial goals are a necessity, because bills are inevitable!

I have to share this bit of information that I was privileged enough to find out. I feel some type of way about it and how it made me better my life choices and spending habits. Zappos is an online shoe store with thousands of brands. The owner is worth $840 million, but he only has FOUR pairs of shoes himself! I don't know what that just did for you, but it made me realize how much unnecessary spending I do—especially on shoes. It also made me realize how much more I could be saving and/or investing, because my shoes aren't cheap!

To wrap this one up quickly, it's nobody else fault that yo' ass is broke! You're the one responsible for the financial situation you're in. Think about this. If you die right now and your debt is out of control, your bills will be left for your loved ones to deal with. But, if you've been financially responsible, your assets will be split among your loved ones!

In short, your finances are *your* responsibility. Managing your finances well is a necessity when it comes to your survival, and ultimately your happi-

ness (no one is happy with a bunch of debt hang-
ing over their heads). So, when it comes to any and
every situation concerning YOUR finances, then
YOU make sure that YOU take control and...

CHAPTER 6

MINDSET

I've noticed that a lot of people attribute their mindsets to their environments. This makes no sense to me at all! How many people nowadays die in the same town, and maybe even the same house, where they've always lived? My point is, life takes you places and the earth is constantly moving, so why would you sit still or base your mindset completely on the position you're currently in? There's so much to see in life, so we should all get out there and live a fulfilling life instead of being stuck where you are.

People are stuck because they have a stuck mindset. People are poor because they have a poor mindset, and people are unhappy because they have an unhappy mindset! It all starts in the mind. There is a saying that you can take the person out of the environment but you can't expect their behavior that they exhibited in the old envi-ronment to change just because their environ-ment did. You've heard "You can take the girl out the hood/ghetto/trailer park but you can't take the hood/ghetto/trailer park out the girl"! Well the reason that saying resonates with us is because it's so universally understood and true, in a lot of cases. This is why I said it all starts in the mind!

The body follows where the head leads it, so you need to realize that your mind leads your life! Your mindset guides your thoughts and manip-ulates your body. If you think you're valuable, then you'll dress and move like you're valuable. Whereas people with low esteem are more likely to be victims who are taken advantage of and live a poor lifestyle.

Your body will tell the world what you're thinking whether you say it or not! Body lan-guage is over ninety percent of communication amongst humans! Look at yourself in the mir-ror and ask yourself what your body language is saying to the world. What are you saying to your co-workers, your boss or your employees? What are you saying to strangers? What are you saying to your pets and children? What are you saying to your significant other and new the people you are attempting to get to know? What's more, what are you saying to and about yourself?

Understand that only you represent you, and your mindset is represented in your body language and recognized in your communication with others. A couple of old sayings illustrate this: "Your handshake ain't matchin' ya smile" and "The eyes are the window to the soul." My point in those examples is people have tried to hide their emotions and mindset for years but that just means they're being untrue to themselves. They're detached from reality and find it impossible to be truly happy. Once again, if you're not honestly happy with and by yourself, then you'll find it impossible to be truly happy with anyone else!

I think it should be clear to you by now why it's so important to have an honest, healthy and happy mindset. Let's be clear about what to claim in order to acquire that kind of mindset so you're not blaming your issues on others or your past. Remember, like Mr. Woodcock said, "We're already past our past, that's why it's called the past!"

We know we can't change the past, so how can we be happy despite whatever horrific or traumatic experience happened to us? It's simple — focus on and invest in the future, while enjoying the gift which is known as the present! The second step toward happiness is continuing to have goals and work to accomplish them. This is part of investing in your future!

When acknowledging your past, don't keep making people villians and victims in your story. Doing this will mean that you constantly victimize yourself too. Move on and forgive. You don't have to forget (well you will when you're ready but I'm not touching on that), but you do have to let go of the bad feelings. What I'm saying is that you have more important and pressing issues to spend your energy on — like achieving your goals. The more you focus on them and ignore the past, the more you'll be in a positive and progressive mindset!

I believe I've been clear about why it's so important to control your mindset by claiming it instead of blaming it on others and your past. I'll say it again —

CHAPTER 7

KIDS

I know kids are a very sensitive and fragile subject but I had to touch on it. As individuals, everybody has a story and history, so obviously don't take any of this personally. I'm talking about children as an idea and a truth. I will only be dealing in the facts, and no emotions will be used in this explanation. I ask that you don't judge me as a human, my family or my upbringing. In America there are laws and rights in the majority of the states regarding children, and that's what I'll be using as my reference for this chapter. Hopefully you are ready to hear the truth and can control your emotions and accept these truths as the facts that they are.

Now that we have all that out of the way, I can honestly say that America offers a plethora of options that allow you not to have custody of, have the responsibility for, or legal association with your child! I will explain all of these options and opportunities that both males and females have from an honest and legal stand point.

How to NOT Have a Child – Just for Men

We all know that children are a result of sex, so the obvious way not to have children is to not have sex. Yes, abstinence is the first defense against having a child. Next is any other form of sex that doesn't end in the penis ejaculating into the vagina, which is what creates the life. Examples of this are endless. With this in mind you can obviously do anal or oral sex, there are male and female condoms as well as birth control pills! I'm sure there's another whole list of options, but this book isn't about sex it's about claiming and not blaming. So, take responsibility if you do not want to have a child.

Now is when I'd like to separate the responsibilities, claiming and blaming. Guys, you can get oral, wear a condom, let her get a female condom, do anal, or some guys say pull out but that's not a method I would suggest, since studies have shown some women can still get pregnant from precum. So, your mission, goal and responsibility is to NOT cum in the vagina IF you don't want a child, plain and simple! Because after the child arrives, YOU have no control or legal options. Your fate, future, and finances are tied to other people from that point on.

Now MY question for all of the fellas out there is WHY?! Why would you give away the power that you have over your freedom, finances, future and your fate? Some of you are saying, "Come on, Lefty, is it that serious?" Uh yeah, it is. Let me show you just how serious it is.

Your fate and future are determined by if she decides to have the baby, or she might not even tell you about it, which is her right and responsibility. Therefore, you can't guarantee any future moves or even options for yourself because you're limited to what she decides! Claim your seed before it turns into a child. Control where you want your seed to go and who you want it to go to.

If you've already passed this point and you have a child, your freedom will be determined by the situation and how you respond to it. If you have to pay child support and you don't do it, they can take your driver's license and even put you in jail for non-payment. So, there ya go. Take control as a man while you have control.

You are the one naturally and legally responsible for your seed! Don't blame the female for anything, even if it's her fault, because in the beginning there was you with your seed. You made this investment with it, so you will reap what you sow! Plant wisely, young men, but claim your seed and don't blame it.

Don't blame your seed for your situation or your "baby mama" or the state or the government, and please definitely don't blame the man or god/devil/universe/karma! You get out of life what you put in, so beware and be thoughtful with how, when and where you invest your seeds on this earth and in your lifetime. You are responsible legally and literally!

So, this is the last thing I'll direct solely at the guys, but it needs to be the first thing you learn as far as claiming and not blaming kids — the proper way to open, apply, use, and discard a condom!

How to NOT Have a Child— for the Ladies

Now ladies, oh yeah, it's your turn, so let's knock it out the park. It's easy with these options and opportunities. First let's start with responsibilities! You are first and foremost responsible for yourself. Do not claim and blame your kids for your deflated dreams, unreached goals, post pregnancy body or the guys/places/fun that you missed out on because you're a mom! This book is about claiming your problems and not blaming.

It's time to claim the decision you made to have a child, deal with the situation you're in and move forward with a better and more positive understanding of yourself, the world and life as a whole.

Let's look at the options females have in America, their rights, and responsibilities. What *can* you claim, what *do* you claim? The truth is, females in America know just like the dudes that babies are made when the sperm reaches the egg. So, to eliminate the possibility of conception, they too can choose to abstain from the act of sex. They can also choose to have oral or anal sex, which would make pregnancy impossible. There are also female condoms and male condoms that the female could have/use.

Now this is where it gets tricky, because there are all sorts of variables such as diet, menstrual cycle, etc. involved in determining the effectiveness of many types of birth control. Birth control like the pill, the IUD, the NuvaRing®, Depo injections, etc. all interact with the woman's body. It's also tricky because the girls know when they're utilizing these things, but the guys don't.

Okay, so now we're past the preventive measures, right? … Wrong! That's where interaction with the males ends and choices solely for females begins. In America, we have an over the counter drug available for females that safely and painlessly prevents any pregnancy within 72 hours after having had sex. There are also abortion clinics. (Again, I am not suggesting or promoting any ideas, I am strictly stating the facts about the rights and responsibilities of male and female American citizens who obviously have sex!)

Moving on…As a female citizen who has a baby in the United States can choose to put the baby up for adoption. There are agencies, programs and whole army of people dedicated to finding children great homes with responsible and able law-abiding adults who will take care of the child.

Now, what's the point in all of this if this is not a sex ed book? Well, I'll tell you. There is no reason to blame your kids for anything, because it is unreasonable, irresponsible and makes no sense. Your kids were your choices! So, *claim them and don't blame them!*

CHAPTER 8

EDUCATION

N ews flash — your parents, the schools and your teachers lied to you! If you're reading this book, then I can safely presume you know that Christopher Columbus did not discover this land that we call America! I'm not going to sit here and list all of the rumors and lies and whatever else that comes along with the misinformation we've been taught in American schools, both public and private, because that's not what this book is about. This book, once again, is about claiming and not blaming things in our lives.

So, since we agree and understand that we've been misinformed, now is the time to unlearn and re-educate ourselves! I suggest that you educate yourself about everything you choose to talk about or be involved in. I'm talking about anything from sex to sports. Be slower to talk and quicker to listen, so that you can learn faster and more effectively.

Claim the attempts and accomplishments that you've made for yourself since realizing that you were being lied to, misinformed and miseducated! What steps have you taken? What have you Googled? What elders have you interviewed and or double-checked things with? I suggest you to talk to your grandparents and oldest living relatives and ask them about their siblings, parents and grandparents! Find out who you are and whose you are like my G-Ma used to say to me! Educate yourself on yourself first, and then on the things that you're interested in.

Research and Learn

Research and educate yourself so you can reach your goals! When I say educate, I don't necessarily mean just school. I always remind people that here in America that there are many sources of free education, including libraries and their computers and books, internet and Google, just to name a few! In other words, there is no excuses for ignorance!

Most of you have learned the ins and outs of social media and spend a lot of your time there. But how many of you know a second language or have a passport? My point is that you're educated about what's going on in other people's lives but you haven't invested in your own!

Education is the key that opens so many doors. What are you educated in and what's the quality of that education? Meaning, how many truthful facts and how much provable/applicable information do you have about any given subject? Let's take it to a more personal level. You know who has had a baby by who, but do you know all the parents and grandparents? Do your kids know all of their grandparents, aunts, uncles and cousins? See what I'm saying? Self-education is also pivotal in all aspects of your life.

Education is also important to your livelihood and for survival! Have you ever heard of the term financial education? Do you know what the "cash flow quadrant" is?! If not, then like I said earlier, get to those libraries, Google and the internet and learn something!"

Having an education of self leads to an understanding of life. Blaming the people who educated you, when you have access to all the information in the world is pointless and a waste of your energy and time! Same goes for blaming your parents. You should realize that your parents were educated the same way you were, but didn't have the many easily accessible sources of knowledge available to them that you have today. It's critical for you to re-educate yourself and share the different truths and facts you've discovered.

Claim the education that you choose and invest in it. Then find like-minded people so you can build off one another. To start this whole re-education process, you have to be willing to be honest about the education you currently possess and be able to...

CHAPTER 9

OUTLOOK

Outlook is actually the polar opposite of mindset, and a lot of people don't know the difference. This is why I separated these ideas into two chapters! Your mindset is what you're thinking and feeling — an internal situation, but your outlook is more your perception of life as a whole — things going on outside of yourself.

This is where optimism and pessimism come in to play. The easiest way to explain those understandings is a glass filled half way. What is your perception of that glass? Is it half empty or does it look half full to YOU? This simple test measures your outlook on life.

I learned the definitions of optimistic and pessimistic in second or third grade, and made my choice right then that the world is half full. I decided this because the earth is over 70% full of water, which makes the glass that we dwell in (earth) over half full! I know I say it so simply, but you have to choose to understand right now that life really can be simple… as simple as you make it. Everything in your life is *your* choice.

Your perception equates to your quality of life! If you perceive the world as a miserable, evil place, then your life will be spent believing you are in that environment and you'll likely be miserable. If you look at the world as a beautiful, amazing collection of mystical beauty and endless treasures, then you will spend your life in a land of wonderfully endless positive possibilities! Claim your outlook in life and then stick to it!

You can look at all of the negatives and evils of the world and be supremely unhappy or you can choose to see the beauty in the world and find joy in your life. Have you ever counted the colors in a sunset or the different shades of green in the grass or the different kinds of trees around you? Probably not, but I bet you've complained or heard someone complain about global warming and how mankind is ruining the planet. See what I'm saying? It's your choice how you see the world, who you surround yourself with and what you talk about. So, keep yourself more than half full with positivity by having not only a positive mindset but also a positive outlook!

You ever notice that "crazy" people seem to smile and laugh a lot? They've found a way to enjoy something that nobody else can see or understand. Take a second and think about this… sane people try to figure out what's going on with the people they classify as "crazy" but the "crazy" people just wanna be left alone or hang around with like-minded individuals. Think about that.

Animals aren't interested in humans, they are interested in survival! So why are humans concerned about so many things that don't make them happy and are counterproductive to their survival? My answer is simple and familiar: misery loves company!

When you choose to have a self-invested mindset and a positive outlook, then you won't see failure because there won't be failure! There will be no losses, just lessons! When you are truly laser focused on hitting your goal, then you'll eventually hit it, but you're not failing during the time you take getting there, you're attempting! So, as long as you have a goal, then you're attempting to hit it. How can you ever fail if you're always headed toward hitting another goal?!

Without failure, your self-image will be much more powerful. After you see yourself and the world in a bright, positive light full of beautiful opportunities, people will see you in that same light. How you see/treat yourself is how others will see/treat you.

This point is where life gets eerily revealing! Not all the people in your life will be motivated by your positivity, because not everyone will share your outlook. You can be your naturally beautiful, healthy, happy self with a great positive mindset, but you cannot make your friends or family change their outlook on life. That's their choice to make.

Dealing with Negativity Positively

When you choose a positive outlook, don't shy away from problems because all problems are opportunities waiting for a solution! In mathematics, the larger amount retains its status, meaning you have to be more positive than somebody else's negative.

Almost a decade ago now, I had a best friend named Miss Lena (STILL a great and lifelong friend of mine). I studied this beautifully bright, wonderfully shining beacon of light and I got to understand her outlook on life. Her name, Alina, means beautiful sunshine, and that's what she CHOSE to be! We confided in one another quite often. She told me some the things that made her sad, but then showed me how to absorb positivity in order to combat the ugliness in this world. She got me to start volunteering and proved to me that is was "good for your soul." This is when I came to understand that YOUR outlook is YOUR choice!

If you're happy with yourself but others aren't, they'll bring their negativity with them everywhere. You just need to have an amount of positivity large enough to overwhelm and overpower their negativity. This is why it's important to observe and take in all the beauty in nature and share it with the humans who choose to be negative.

Laughter is contagious and so are smiles. The same has been said about crime. This means the intermediate truth is that people are influenced by other people. So, what you have to decide as a human is how your life will be influenced by others and how you'll use your positive outlook to influence others.

Some people dress up and hide their hurt, anger, addiction, etc. That's because they are not happy with who they have chosen to be. They are still in blame mode, which is full of negativity. You can't help them change their outlook until they decide they want to do it.

Haters

Don't let a "hater" mess up your view of life. I'd like to dive into that a little more in detail. You are choosing to be focused and positive in your life, but that doesn't mean that others are. They may even actively try to sabotage your positivity. You must eliminate this threat!

You cannot battle every negative you come across because you'd lose focus on the positives in your life. Understand that everybody is an individual and respect them and life as such. Your life is your time on earth from your view, but understand that there are many perspectives besides yours. With that in mind, don't get lost wading through negativity brought on by others, stay focused on your path to happiness!

Remember we're still in the head right now because the head controls the body! Brain equals mindset, which will control how you are seeing out of your eyes and allow you to "stop and smell the roses."

Next is what you choose to say and your body language, which we've already discussed communicates your feelings to the world without you even saying a word. Your words and actions need to be just as positive and goal oriented as your thoughts. It's a complete package.

Getting Real

Blaming your outlook on someone else is like blaming how your eyes see the world on someone else. You need to understand how implausible and unreasonably pathetic it is for a grown-up adult to think that someone else could ever be responsible for how you see the world! Read the sentence again. Glad we can all laugh together.

How you see the world is YOUR choice and that world vision is reinforced by what you do and who you associate with. Some people see Elvis as a captivating entertainer and others see him as a copycat and a thief — it's all in the individual's perspective. If you don't like what you're seeing in yourself, change it. Look for the beauty in life — even death can be beautiful, think autumn leaves.

I hope that you all now know why it is imperative, when it comes to your outlook, that you...

CHAPTER 10

POSITIVITY

A s I touched on briefly in the last chapter, mathematically speaking, you have to possess a higher amount of positivity to overpower the negativity that a problem presents to you for the end result to remain positive. Soak up the sun and feel the positivity of the world and nature.

Ponder this one for a tick: when have you ever seen something non-human (sunset, rainbow, cloud formation, hummingbird, etc.) and been upset or had an exchange (smelled a flower, heard a bird sing) and been disappointed or pissed off? Now, how many times has this been the case with humans? Now that the tally has been taken, I'm sure you get my point. Bring in the positivity and beauty from non-humans to not only share with other humans but also to use as a tool to build patience, smiles and positive energy.

You Are Your Own Force

Sometimes when you're happy, people just wanna test your battery and see how much energy you have, even when they have no interest or use for you or your energy. Remember, you're the one who gets to decide how much of your positive energy you want to invest into any situation or person.

One thing that vexes me more than anything else is people who blame their negativity on others! "I'm so negative because that's all I've heard or been around." ... I call bullshit! You're the one who's creating the negativity! You are your own force and you control your own energy. You're the one who decides if your energy is negative or positive!

Here's a great example of claiming/blaming. You're eating well and feeling wonderful, but you give credit for your great health choices to Jared, the former spokesperson for Subway sandwiches. Suddenly Jared's whole debacle is exposed, which makes you lose faith in him. You stop eating healthy, and blame it on Jared. If you'd only claimed your choices as your own and not attached them to someone else, you'd probably still be eating healthy foods, regardless of what the sandwich spokesman did.

Don't give others power over your positivity. Everyone is an individual and should be making their own life choices to control how and what they invest in, as well as how they spend their time on earth. You spend your whole life being you, so choose to claim every part of your life. Take control and make it happen for yourself by claiming your choices and decisions and not blaming them on others. Blaming someone else for anything positive in your life that was a direct effect of the choices and decisions that you made gives others more power over your life than you choose to have.

Only when you are ready to be a healthy and happy grown-up adult will you choose to take charge and actually do it. I can't make you brave, but I can arm you with the truth — what you choose to allow is what will happen.

So, when it comes to your positivity, you cannot blame your positivity or lack thereof on anybody else. What can you do instead of blaming it? Of course, you can and should, claim it! Claiming your positivity means claiming the process it takes to be, and remain, positive.

This brings us back to investing in your own positivity and banking it, like counting your blessings! You're reading this book, so obviously you want to improve yourself and your situation. You can make the changes needed to turn your life around to positivity. Remember, you have so many things to be thankful for and positive about!

There are many positive people out there who have what you might consider less than you do. Don't feel sorry for them, learn from them. Consider the difficulties Ray Charles and Stevie Wonder have faced in their lives, and then look at how they've overcome them and achieved amazing success.

It's time to step up your game and remember you have NO excuse for not being positive and ultimately successful! When it comes to your positivity you must...

CHAPTER 11

ENERGY

Your energy is a lot like your positivity, but is more encompassing. Control your energy by claiming it. There is and will be both negative energy and positive energy surrounding your life, but claiming yours and not blaming it is about moving on with your life.

Have you ever seen an entertainer, whether it be a musician, comedian or vocalist, do something called "turn the room"? What that term refers to is manipulating the crowd's emotions with your energy, through both your presence and your performance. A comic might tell one joke that turns the crowd against them, some celebrities make one comment and lose their following, and some rappers and athletes make one mistake and the public/society turns on them. This happens to non-celebrities too. Sometimes, it only takes one thing to change people's perception of you.

You, as an individual, are responsible for what you say and do. You have to take charge of your life and stop simply following others and letting them control your narrative! Your energy is something *you* have to claim in all situations.

Remember, even if you claim it and have good intentions, sometimes you can be wrong. When that happens, you have to possess a certain amount of honesty and humility and admit that you're wrong. Always remember that nobody is perfect, so in life there will be times where you are wrong! Welcome these times and appreciate them as opportunities to learn and better yourself. You don't and can't have all the answers. By claiming your energy, you can say "Oops I thought you meant this…" or find out where you got mistaken or misunderstood, learn the correct answer and better yourself.

Claiming your energy also allows you to do exactly that … claim your energy, meaning you will be a more empowered being. You'll be stronger in self; therefore, others can't hurt you, bring you down or hold you back. Things from your past, guilt, feelings of inadequacy or even debt will hold no power over you. You'll feel tremendous self-worth and self-value, which will lead to prominent self-esteem and good self-image. Having confidence in who you are and what you're doing in life will give you the energy to do uncommon things here on earth.

The Wright brothers had to believe before trying to fly. They made up their minds, they put the energy into it and they defied gravity! You, too, can achieve greatness with a positive mindset, outlook, and energy! Claiming your energy is finding your peace and not separating from it.

Here are two beautiful gems you'll be able to polish over and over and eventually appreciate and hold as valuable assets: everything doesn't need a reaction and everything doesn't require an immediate response.

I'm sure that it's clear now that when it comes to your energy a necessary step in the process of your growth, maturity, success and life is that you...

CHAPTER 12

HEALTH

This will be a quick, simple but significant chapter due to the title of the book. Seriously, how much would or could I teach you about not blaming your health on anybody else? Now that I type it, I do know a lot of people say their health issues are hereditary, without claiming the behavior that caused the issues. Hope I didn't lose you on that one, I'll go in depth.

A lot of people blame their family, genes or their parents for the state of their health, but they have never taken control of their own situation, done the research, or invested the time, effort, money and sacrifices needed to change and do better. You can blame diabetes and high blood pressure on the people that came before you, but fail to blame their poor diet and nonexistent exercise regimens. You have to claim your health to change it, better it and sustain it.

There are two closely related major health categories — mental and physical. Your mental health oftentimes effects and even controls your physical health. Have you ever heard, "Kill the head and the body will die"? I know you have, lol. So, same principle applies here: if you invest in your mental health then you will in turn be investing in your physical health.

The human brain needs oxygen and blood in order to operate properly. The better the brain operates and the more blood and oxygen it gets, the better the heart, lungs and other vital organs will operate. This is common knowledge, so I suggest you research things that hinder oxygen and blood flow, and then find out what promotes oxygen and blood flow. Once you know this, start investing in those foods, drinks and healthy activities.

If you put the best into your body, you will get the best out. You might even realize that meat is non-essential to your healthy body. What you put in, is what you get out, or as the bible says, "you will reap what you sow." So, invest wisely when it comes to your health.

Claim what works for you to be the best and healthiest you can be. Don't blame your poor diet or health on how you were raised or where you're from or your kids or significant other, etc. You have nothing and nobody else to blame your poor health on — because it's all up to you. These are your choices!

If you work out because working out is free — that is a choice! If you choose to put everything unhealthy into your body, then why are you even reading this chapter?! Your health is all up to you.

We live in a country where healthy food, plants, and vitamins and minerals can be delivered to your door. Use those free library computers and Google to learn what's healthy for you. There are no excuses as to why you can't invest in your own health and the education you need to learn how to be healthier.

Don't let negativity, fast food commercials, friends who tempt you with unhealthy treats, etc. knock you off your path. Keep it pushing and stay focused on your positivity and healthy mindset, so you can keep your positive outlook on life.

Healthy is good, don't let anyone lie to you. This doesn't just refer to your body. A healthy wallet and a healthy bank account go right along with a healthy mind and a healthy body to help you create an overall healthy lifestyle. These should all be goals of yours as a grown-up adult. So, when it comes to your health...

CHAPTER 13

GOALS

The majority of Americans have had one common goal for decades — the Golden Rule! Come on you all know it, say it out loud: treat others the way you want to be treated! That comes from a bible verse: "do onto others as you would have them do onto you."

Let's really take time to understand this Golden Rule before we start digging into claiming not blaming our goals.

I'll explain two things simply, because I don't want anyone to think that I'm attacking the bible in any way, shape, form or fashion. First things first, I have told you where the saying comes from, so understand that treating someone the way you want to be treated is not what the saying really means. Treating someone the way you want to be treated literally makes no sense, because nobody else is you! If you are cold and someone else is hot, but you control the thermostat — then taking the Golden Rule literally, you would turn the thermostat down so they can cool off. The true meaning of the saying is to be mindful of another person's situation and point of view, not take things literally. In other words, don't treat people like you want to be treated because they are not you — treat people with respect and they will do the same for you.

Setting New Goals

While attempting to live by the Golden Rule is a great goal, you need some new ones in your life too. In order to set new goals, you need to understand some new things. So, let's get some things understood!

Sometimes, people set goals that they don't really understand. So, the first thing we wanna do when setting our new goals is think things through. Hopefully all of you reading this have already read my first book, *Girlz R S-too-pid & Boyz R Duh-m,* but if you didn't then first of all, shame on you! Lol. Just kidding! Seriously, catch up.

Your new goals need to be realistic, not some fantasy you've got 'cause your parents told you you're a prince/princess. That just won't happen for you. There ain't no Santa Clause either! In short, your parents lied to you! Get over it!

Now don't go blaming ya parents, like "Oh they ruined me. They told me I was special, but I'm not and it fucked me up!" Quit being a little bitch-ass victim, gets ya nuts up! Now's the time to grow up and start "adulting"! Claim your goals, because there is nobody else to blame for them!

Educate yourself and take control of your life. Set realistic goals and get the information needed to achieve them. Change your mindset and out-look! Dedicate yourself to being the best version of yourself by investing in yourself — your health, your diet, your hygiene, your wellness, your value.

Get your personal life straight. Be the best son, daughter, niece, nephew, aunt, uncle, mom, dad, grandparent, godparent, etc. that you can be. Start your goals by putting your family first, then move on to school, business and other interests.

Learn as much as you can, and be sure to be a great listener! The voice of experience is always a great teacher. While you're learning, play it smart. Keep yourself healthy so that your brain works at high capacity. Stay hydrated with alkaline water, exercise regularly, eat a healthy, electric diet and take regular stretch breaks when working at the computer.

When you're educated about your goals and healthy enough to achieve them, you'll be able to communicate your dreams to others. This might result in building a network and team of other positive and healthy individuals who have the same goals. Therefore, resulting in a healthy, positive and successful life for you.

Now that you've learned how to set a goal and achieve it, there's no limit to the things you can do, as long as you continue to follow the same process each time!

Just so we're clear about this goal process...

CHAPTER 14

OUTCOME

Y ou are an outcome. You are a product. You are a solution. You are a person! Children are products of their environment. When you were born, you were a solution to the equation: one male + one female = you. Yes, you are the solution, the product, and the outcome of your parents procreation! A pro created you! You are unique. You are special. You are an individual!

The key to your successful outcome is unlocking your individualism and finding your superpower, if you will. Doing this will allow you to control your own outcomes in life. The only way to do this is to be honest with yourself, get to know yourself, be yourself and better yourself constantly and consistently.

You already are a product of your environment. When you're young, the environment is your household, as you get older, it's your school, then it moves on to your community, city, state, and country. This, limited yet hopefully rapidly widening, perspective of life has shaped who you are, what you believe and how you think.

When you are young, you are both a product and a solution, and others will invest in training and shaping you into who you will become. When you become an adult and take control of your life, you relinquish all blame and trade it for understanding. You use the foundation others built for you as a formal background, accepting it as part of your history and utilizing the experiences to build yourself and become strong.

Since you're now a grown-up adult, it's time for you to research and expand your knowledge of the things you know, and find other things to become interested in. These may be things you need, things that assist in your survival, such as financial planning information and proper health, diet and exercise. Now that your grown and educated, you are not only a product, but you're also a solution — for your spouse, children, parents, grandparents and others. In my opinion, if your family took care of you for 18 years, then I think you should repay the favor at some point — but that's just me. After all, you are the sum of the product of their meeting and connection on this earth in this lifetime.

On top of being the product and solution, of course I also mentioned that you are the outcome. You are the outcome of your perspective, your education, and your experiences. Today is the outcome of yesterday and all days before, so if you want a better or different outcome then you can and should invest in having it! Put in what you want back out, it's your life and you only get one to live.

Remember that every second is irreplaceable. There is no time to waste on negative people and things that aren't good for you and don't help you to build a better future. When you're bored or watching TV or thinking about putting something unhealthy in your body, just say to yourself, "It's totally free to focus on me!" Then do something that's good for you — push-ups or sit-ups, Google a new city to visit or a fact about the city you live in currently! Use your time to better yourself by learning a new language, researching your family history by talking an elder about the way things were when they were growing up.

Find out as much as you can about yourself and your situation in order to better yourself and your situation. Investing in yourself is not self-ish — it is necessary! The outcome from working out routinely and eating right is a healthier life due to proper blood and oxygen flow to the brain and body, another outcome from this same activity is you look and feel great and have more positive energy!

Focus your brain on positive outcomes, like the lasting impressions you make and leave on people. What will be the outcome of your education, your family, your presence, your existence, your life, your time on this earth? Who you are and why you are here will be determined by what you do for yourself and others. So, schedule your outcomes by setting goals. Remember that your outcome and what you become is all up to you! So...

CHAPTER 15

FUTURE

I f you've read my first book, then I'm confident you are an honest, educated, responsible individual. If you have not read it, then you should. Read it, then come back and read this book again so you will get the full benefit of what I'm telling you.

Being an honest and responsible individual, I have no doubt that you are able to claim your past and not blame it on anybody else after reading and understanding the first chapter in this book. There is nothing you can do to change your past, so there's no use trying to blame it on someone else. It's your past and yours alone.

The past has already happened, so we have to focus on the future and what you can do to turn around the life you're living right now. You can only go forward in life, so don't miss precious

CLAIM IT! DON'T BLAME IT!

moments of this gift known as the present by steady looking to the past!

The Serenity Prayer by Reinhold Niebuhr illustrates this well, and might be something to recite to yourself to help you to look to the future.

God, grant me the serenity to accept
the things I cannot change,
the courage to change the things that I can,
and the wisdom to know the difference.
Living one day at a time,
accepting hardships as the pathway to peace,
taking, as He did, this sinful world as it is,
not as I would have it…"

Understanding and living this prayer will provide you more peace than any single experience in your life. I guarantee! Learn it, live it, and encode it into your DNA! This understanding will free your mind and open it to the present. It will open the path to planning for your future by letting go of your past. Letting go of your past leads to forgiveness, because you won't be holding onto hurt, pain and bitterness, instead you'll have hope and motivation to plan for the future.

Stay in the realm of reality, and it should be easy to stick to what that prayer asks you to do. Use it to help free yourself from addiction, and to help you mend relationships and so you can find new, healthy, positive ones! You'll have love in your life and maybe even a love life if you have the time. You'll not only feel successful, but you'll be successful.

Once you've left your past behind and mended your relationships, claim your finances so you'll have the freedom and time to focus on your mindset and keeping it positive. Claim your kids and appreciate them, instead of blaming them. Become fully invested in new, more relevant education and information, and keep it all positive. Invest all of that positivity into your energy and carry it with you in the world.

Become a healthy individual, claiming and achieving your goals, bettering yourself and controlling your outcome. Take charge of your life, and manifest your future by applying this one simple understanding…

A SPECIAL THANK-YOU

Special thanks to all of the essential workers out there — from health care to first responders, nurses, and doctors to the radio DJs, pastors, news casters and reporters keeping us ALL up to speed and soothing our concerns during this unprecedented time.

My thanks also extend to fast food and telecommunication workers, customer service people, and all of the volunteers who donated their time. I love you all and you are all appreciated!

I'll bet most of you hated your jobs before, but now that you know you are real heroes you'll have more reason than ever to be proud of yourself and your position in life as an essential worker.

Whatever you do, wherever and whoever you are, please *claim it, don't blame it!*

ABOUT THE AUTHOR

Ray Lefty Rhodes, now officially Lord Ray Lefty Rhodes, is owner/operator of ten companies — two more than when his first book was released. He also graduated simultaneously from Ashworth University (with honors) for travel and tourism, and from the historical Fashion Institute of Technology in Manhattan during the summer of 2020 (amidst the COVID pandemic). He is now taking on the world of design as well as continuing his entrepreneurial enterprises, where he's had a myriad of accomplishments Leading by example, his goal is to provide a step-by-step mental path to happiness and success!

www.ingramcontent.com/pod-product-compliance
Lightning Source LLC
Chambersburg PA
CBHW060244030426
42335CB00014B/1594